THE SHADOW KNOWS

Adrian Mitchell

The Shadow Poet Laureate

THE SHADOW KNOWS

POEMS 2000–2004

ERIC BLOODAXE

BLOODAXE BOOKS

ISBN: 1 85224 664 2

First published 2004 by
Bloodaxe Books Ltd,
Highgreen,
Tarset,
Northumberland NE48 1RP.

www.bloodaxebooks.com
For further information about Bloodaxe titles
please visit our website or write to
the above address for a catalogue.

Bloodaxe Books Ltd acknowledges
the financial assistance of
Arts Council England, North East.

Cover printing by J. Thomson Colour Printers Ltd, Glasgow.

Printed in Great Britain by
Cromwell Press Ltd, Trowbridge, Wiltshire.

To all those who work for peace
especially my own family and friends
and all those who took part,
on February 15th, 2003,
in the greatest demonstration against war
that the world has ever known
so far

ACKNOWLEDGEMENTS

Poems in *The Shadow Knows* have previously appeared in *Red Pepper*, *Peace News*, *Poetry Review*, *Camden New Journal*, *The Guardian*, *The Independent* and *Poetry Scotland*. They have been broadcast on BBC Radio 4's *Today* programme and on the BBC World Service. They have been performed at many poetry gigs and demonstrations – including events organised by the Stop the War Coalition, The Medical Foundation for the Victims of Torture, Poets Against the War etc.

Page 12: 'The Shadow Knows' by Jerry Leiber and Mike Stoller, © 1958 (Renewed) Jerry Leiber Music & Mike Stoller Music. International copyright secured. All rights reserved. Used by permission.

THE SHADOW POET LAUREATE'S WARNING TO EDUCATIONAL INSTITUTIONS

None of the work in this or any of my other books is to be used in connection with any examination or test whatsoever. If you like a poem of mine, learn it, recite it, sing it or dance it – in a school or wherever you happen to be. But don't force anyone to study it or write a boring essay about it. This is the first step in The Shadow Poet Laureate's scheme to destroy the examination systems of the world, which have made true education almost impossible.

The Shadow would like to remind all students who are not happy that there is no law which compels them to attend school – so long as it can be proved that they are being educated satisfactorily. (Contact Education Otherwise for information and help.)

CONTENTS

William Blake Says:
Every Thing That Lives Is Holy

Long live the Child
Long live the Mother and Father
Long live the People

Long live this wounded Planet
Long live the good milk of the Air
Long live the spawning Rivers and the mothering Oceans
Long live the juice of the Grass
and all the determined greenery of the Globe

Long live the Elephants and the Sea Horses,
the Humming-birds and the Gorillas,
the Dogs and Cats and Field-mice –
all the surviving Animals
our innocent Sisters and Brothers

Long live the Earth, deeper than all our thinking

we have done enough killing

Long live the Man
Long live the Woman
Who use both courage and compassion
Long live their Children

The SHADOW in WARTIME

The Shadow Knows

You can hide down in the alley
With your hat pulled over your eyes
You can wear a wig or mustache
Or any old disguise
You can change your name an' address
Even change your style of clothes
But the Shadow knows
The Shadow knows…

You thought you had me baffled
You thought I didn't know
But I know where you're goin', baby,
Long before you go
You can't even snap your fingers
Or wiggle your toes
Without the Shadow knows
The Shadow knows

Now baby, stop your jivin'
And your messin' round
Because I know what you're puttin'
Long before you put it down
You better mind your P's and Q's
And your M's an' N's an' O's
Because the Shadow knows
The Shadow knows

JERRY LEIBER & MIKE STOLLER

The Shadow Poet Laureateship

The official elegy for Princess Margaret was the final straw. There had to be an antidote: a poet who would stalk the powerful and the pretentious. The socialist magazine *Red Pepper* invited Adrian Mitchell to don the dreaded costume of The Shadow Poet Laureate and write regular poems for their columns. At a midnight ceremony in a Stoke Newington crossword den frequented by swarthy anarchist stokers, he was anointed with tomato ketchup. Then he was decked in the scarlet and red cloak, the charcoal sombrero and the Parisian blue suede shoes which are the garb of the Shadow. From his interview with intrepid Jane Shallice, we excerpt the following:

JS: *You are the people's first Shadow Poet Laureate, but you come from an honourable tradition.*

SHADOW: Yes, like Lord Byron and William Blake, both of whom wrote wonderful Shadow poetry. Byron particularly aimed his at Southey, when Southey was Poet Laureate. He wrote some marvellous stuff aimed at people like Castlereagh and mad King George; Blake wrote against kings and warriors and priests. There have always been Shadow Poet Laureates, but I'm the first to take it on as a mission.

Somebody, wearing a sort of Spanish cape and a dark hat, needs to be standing just behind the Poet Laureate, leering. To remind him that he's human and even the Royal Family are human. But I don't want to concentrate my fire on the Royals, but on the rich and powerful, those who rule and ruin this world and keep leading us into wars.

JS: *And your inspiration?*

SHADOW: For instance – I found out that Tony Blair, like all British Prime Ministers, has to write a letter, which is sealed and given to the captains of all our Trident nuclear submarines. They are only allowed to open it when England is destroyed. And they'll know that because the *Today* programme on Radio Four will not have broadcast for four days. Then they can open the envelope. So I wrote Tony Blair's Secret Note...

JS: *How did you come to write your challenge to the Poet Laureate – 'Unjubilee Poem' – which was published in the* Guardian *in February 2002?*

SHADOW: The *Guardian* had just published some sycophantic pieces about the present Laureate. I kept meeting non-poets who said that he was 'an ambassador for Poetry'. Well I don't think Poetry needs Ambassadors or any other kind of diplomat. There are career poets in every generation. You can see how many committees they are on, how many things they edit. It's important to pull the plug on them. Free the baby and the bathwater! Poets shouldn't take titles except ridiculous ones like the Shadow. And anyone can have that. When young poets complain they're not getting recognition I tell them they can be Shadow Poet Laureates too! What poets need is a democratic trades union and wages for good work. I won't be spending my time dogging Andrew Motion's footsteps. My little squib wasn't personal - it was about his work as Laureate.

JS: *May we hear it again, Shadow?*

SHADOW: If you insist.

Unjubilee Poem

Liquid sunshine gushing down
To dance and sparkle on the Crown.
I see the Laureate's work like this:
A long, thin streak of yellow piss.

Anti-Establishment Poet Is Difficult, Court Told

Totally thrilled by my appointment as Shadow Poet Laureate and the world-wide media reaction to same, I was disconcerted to be asked – before my costume was even delivered, to react to the passing of the Queen Mother. Not only was *Red Pepper* intrigued to catch my reaction – but the revolutionary *Evening Standard* wanted to reprint my reaction. (£1,000 plus VAT is my fee, *Evening Standard*).

When I was elected Poet Laureate, thirty years ago, I made two conditions for my acceptance:

1. I would appear at every Royal Wedding dressed in the costume of a Giant Banana.

2. I would be entitled to tap-dance on the coffin at every Royal Funeral. I am still awaiting a reply. Meanwhile here is:

A Refusal to Write a Royal Elegy

When Kings and Queens decide to die
Up in a golden coach they fly
To Heaven to do Royal things
With the imperial King of Kings.

But write them elegies, you call?
They never touched my life at all.

A boy, I mourned when Roosevelt died.
For Gandhi and Martin Luther King, I cried,
Comedians died – I wept and shook
Milligan, Cooper, Morecambe, Moore and Cook.
 Weeping with grief to see them gone.
 Weeping with joy at how they shone.

 How can I write of royalty
Whose lives are meaningless to me?

Grim Reaper's Last Request:
No More Death Poetry, Please

Gently I float down the dusky river
In my silent boat with grey sails a-quiver
And as you espy my silvery mask
'Who art thou?' you cry, and you may well ask.

For I have of names a multitude,
And many are ghastly and some a bit rude.
Yea, most folk do speak of me under their breath…
Ah yes, you have guessed it, men call me Death!

I am just a poetic personification
Oft employed in your funeral oration.
I have featured in many a woeful ode
On the loss of a Princess or a pet toad.

They are moony poems and moany poems
And poems that make me cringe,
Like the one on the Man at the Gate of the Year,
Which doth creak like a rusty hinge.

And they always end with some anti-Death stuff:
Weep not, neither mourn – he's not dead.
He's not dead? That's all right then, no more of this guff –
Let's go out and paint the town red!

Only Asking

love between strangers
love between animals
love between lovers
love between children

lakes
mountain streams
oceans
fountains
rain and snowfall
all kinds of love

what the fuck
has love got to do
with socialism?

Hot News via Nokia

The Chairman of Surgical Missiles PLC
Paused on his Arabian stallion outside the BBC
As through the mobile poured his secretary's report
Of the invention of the spear and the casualties at Agincourt.

Back to the Happidrome

Everybody's happy at the Happidrome
— OLD RADIO CATCHPHRASE

But when we came round the corner out of
   Paris in the ice cream sunshine –
      There was Colombia in flames
         There was Palestine in flames
           There was Afghanistan in flames
in a backwash tidal monsoon of fire –

at what heat does the hair burn?
at what heat do newspapers burn?
at what heat does flesh burn?
at what heat do the eyeballs boil?
at what heat does the heart explode?
at what heat does the atmosphere burn?

at what heat do the people awake?

   The Army, the Navy and the Royal Marines!
With missiles and gunships and submarines!
   Lords and Commons, Presidents and Queens!
     They all dance hand in hand
With the Arms Manufacturers of this land!

      All singing;
   Want to make a killing in the Congo?
    Pull my bongo!
   Want to make mass-murder in the Middle East?
    Call my beast!
Want to do some big-time fire and sword?
Pull the Armageddon Emergency Cord!
Tear the skin off the face of the human race –
    with British Aerospace
      it gives employment
    with British Aerospace
      you're laughing
    with British Aerospace!

No More War

As War eats more and more of its victims
Growing huge and strong on foreign flesh,
Quiet ladies and gentlemen in grey suits
Will ask you to learn the killing trade.

Maybe you've got no hope of work
And the Army sounds like a steady job
And you've seen Ross Kemp in *Ultimate Force*
Wasting the terrorists. Tell them: No.

As War multiplies and War and its children
Start to devour our own parents and children,
Your friendly postman will hand you an order
To leave your home and go learn to kill.

It's simpler to go when you're told to go.
Maybe you're worried what your family will say.
Maybe you're frightened by their prisons
Designed for crushing men and women. Tell them: No.

Prepare your defence. Explain to them peacefully
Why you refuse to kill or die for them.
Call your witnesses – Martin Luther King
Or Gandhi or Jesus or Buddha
Or your own loving heart.

The Only Necessary Exam

Once a year each citizen is
Scanned for sadistic tendencies.
If you find being cruel is vital
You'll be awarded a public title –
Sir Viper, Ms Iniquity
Or Diabolical Marquis.
This title will remain until
You pass our Courses in Goodwill,
Gentleness and Imagination.
Till then you're barred from any occupation
Which grants power over the body or mind
Of powerless creatures of any kind –
Children, babies, refugees,
The old, the sick, giraffes and chimpanzees,
Prisoners of peace, prisoners of war,
Actor, soldier, nun or whore –
You shan't torment them any more.

Starved of your cowardly enjoyment
You will be found alternative employment
So you can make a mild, fresh start
Playing a totally harmless part –
A TV wrestler, a Hare Rama,
A Leeds footballer, a Saatchi embalmer,
Or, if too useless for all these –
One of those tame New Labour MPs.

Human Beings

(for the company of the truthful and beautiful Red Red Shoes
by Charles Way, staged by the Unicorn Theatre for Children)

look at your hands
your beautiful useful hands
you're not an ape
you're not a parrot
you're not a slow loris
or a smart missile
you're human

not british
not american
not israeli
not palestinian
you're human

not catholic
not protestant
not muslim
not hindu
you're human

we all start human
we end up human
human first
human last
we're human
or we're nothing

nothing but bombs
and poison gas
nothing but guns
and torturers
nothing but slaves
of Greed and War
if we're not human

look at your body
with its amazing systems
of nerve-wires and blood canals
think about your mind
which can think about itself
and the whole universe

        look at your face
which can freeze into horror
        or melt into love
    look at all that life
        all that beauty
        you're human
    they are human
    we are human
let's try to be human

        dance!

**Red Pepper is written by a humane bunch
so buy a dozen copies every munch**
(to Ralph Steadman, painter of the Real World, with love)

press button one for Fire that tears all their skin off
two – Poisons jabbed into the brains of the meek
three – a crowd of Exploding bodies
four – this month's novelty Torture Technique.
the last eight years has seen a great advance
in all kinds of surgical strike,
    but you can order up a lynchmob job
        if that's the kind of thing you like.
    until they press all the buttons at once
we stagger round waist-deep in blood and shite
        Murder and Money rule the world –
and we're still trying to be fucking polite.

So Beautiful

The land is so beautiful
that people forgot about
God and the Devil
and their Great War

People were supposed to be taking sides
and enlisting as soldiers
in that Great War
So God and the Devil
got together
They invented the Hatred Bush
a little twisting
yellow as custard
thorny bush

anyone who brushes past
is scratched by the tiny claws
of the Hatred Bush
and soon he feels the yellow hatred
swimming down his veins
towards his heart

And when he sees anyone
who hasn't been scratched
the yellow hatred liquid
becomes excited under his skin
and the pressure builds
into a murder mood

The land is so beautiful
there had to be trouble
happy people don't pray to God
happy people aren't afraid of the Devil

Middle Easter

seven o'clock on a sunlit morning
　　ambling down a London hillside

wondering how can Palestine and Israel
shake off their terrors and make peace
shake off their leaders and make peace

when a scarlet-headed woodpecker
　　　simply, gracefully,
　　showed me a miracle
flying from one tree to another
　　　with no fear whatsoever

Good Friday, 2002

Tony Blair's secret note sealed in an envelope and given to the captains of Britain's Trident submarines

Dear Skipper,

Ahoy there! This is, or rather was, your Prime Minister and Commander-in-Chief, Tony Blair

As the envelope says: 'This is to be opened only in the case of a massive nuclear attack on the British Isles and the breakdown of all communication with the same.'

By now you will have ensured that the BBC's Radio 4 has failed to provide its *Today* programme for four consecutive days.

So you may be pretty darned sure that I have been, along with Cherie, the boys and the rest of the population of Great Britain, rendered unto dust or similar.

But keep your pecker up! Here are my final orders to you and the other submarine captains.

1. You will now take orders from the Presidential office of the United States of America or the provisional Presidential office operating from an American bunker if the United States of America is still there.
2. If the USA is not still there, you should make your way towards Australia, if Australia is still there.
3. You will decide for yourself, using your heart, brain and patriotic organs, whether or not to aim and fire your British missiles towards the country most likely to have attacked Great Britain.
4. If Australia is not still there, you should probably lurk in the blue depths for forty days and forty nights before surfacing to take a look around.
5. Good luck.

   Yours for freedom and democracy,

The Right Honourable Tony Blair, Prime Minister.

Emergency Ward – U.N. Hospital 2002

into the Ward bursts the Chief Surgeon
eagle-screaming at the top of his voice
and Matron matching him pace for pace
and talking loud into her mobile
and fast stamping over the disinfected lino
and behind those two
a tight pack of Doctors and Nurses
shouting at the patients on each side
and wagging their rubber-gloved fingers
till the Chief Surgeon holds up a hand
and stops dead still
and suddenly everybody stops dead still.

and the Chief Surgeon looks around
Listen up, he says, and listen good –
there's a psycho killer on the loose.
Where?
Right here in our hospital

I know who he is –
he wears a doctor's white coat
but he's no doctor
He's tooken a locked-up office
on the seventh floor
got it jam-packed full of
knives and gas and poisons and other bad stuff.

Very very bad stuff, says Matron.
As soon as he's ready, and he's nearly ready,
that killer is going to use
his knives and gas and poisons other bad stuff
to kill everyone he doesn't like in the Hospital.

Silence.
Silent whispering of
O my God and Fucking Hell.

Come on, says the Chief Surgeon,
let's go kick down his door
take his office apart
and bin his knives and gas and poisons
and other bad stuff.

Silence.
The Chief is talking like a violent drunk
but he hasn't taken a drink for years.

Then a small Doctor from godknowswhere stands up.

There's rules about that, he says.
We search his room, Chief, –
we ought to search your room too.
You've probably got a mess of
knives and gas and poisons and other bad stuff.

Sure I have, says the Chief, but I'm entitled
and I'm not going to use them as far as you know
and if I decide to – that's my concern.

That's the Chief's concern, says the Matron,
come to that I have knives for opening letters
and gas for heating and some of my perfumes
would burn you inside out if you drank them –

But we're peaceful non-psychos, says the Chief,
that's the difference
and that guy up on the seventh floor
is just about to attack everybody in range,
how do I know that?
I understand how homicidal maniacs work.
I have explored the inside of the brains
of this particular madman
and my conclusion is he is poised to spring –
so what do we do?
Kick down his door, jump him, waste him,
burn down his office and blow it up.

At this point a couple of junior Nurses
stand up and start leading
a few of the children from the Burns Ward
out of the ward.

Hey, you, hang on, yells the Chief.
You've got to decide –
is this a hospital for curing the sick
or is it a wonderworking powerful machine
for stamping out all the evil on earth?

Terror Time

The War Against Terror
What does that mean?
War is terror
to the people underneath the
bombs
So call it
The Terror Against Terror
So the world can understand
Your mission here on earth

Take off the Insect Mask,
George W Bush

Have you taken the pills today, Mr President?

It's not easy. Not easy at all.
Having to think.
Keeping your brain from stumbling.
Stopping your anger from blazing.

It's not easy.
There's a black hole inside of you
Screaming for a drink.
Talk in short sentences. Smile and nod.
Hail to the Chief. Amazing.

Then they lead me
Out of the Oval Room
Along the soft carpet
To the green door.

In we go.
My gold cage elevator
Goes down smoothly,
Goes down so smoothly.
Mantovani. Silver strings.

The floor gives a little bump.
Out I go into my den.
My keepers wave goodbye chief.
Goodbye.
Alone at last.

I choose a DVD.
Usually John Wayne.
Then I pick up my palmpad
And press TRAIN.

Out of the wall trundles
A steam engine
Dragging trolleys
Of every kind of drink and mixers –
The Highball Express.
John Wayne rides into town.
Now I am really smiling.

The Operation

hero executioners
forensic psychopaths
extreme venom
storm rockets
   they're all part of
The Operation

born-again dragons
Jurassic porridge
shock wheeltappers
scorpion singers
   all essential to
The Operation

and all you
grizzly crackers
colditz wannabes
boogie hungerbabes
and bungalow maniacs
   you're absolutely central to
The Operation

To the Pre-emptive Air Forces

Men women children animals –
slash them to pieces all alike.
Precision bombing.
Smart missiles.
You are Jack the Ripper
on a surgical strike.

Adult Picture Book

What's in the mirror?
A mask to borrow.
What's in the mirror?
The mists of tomorrow.
What's in the mirror?
Bombed-out Gomorrah.
What's in the mirror?
Silent horror.

Roundabout

A war is born: neighbour kills neighbour,
They kill till they can kill no more.
A peace is signed, war goes into labour
And dies giving birth to another war.

Playground

    dark brown eyes
scanning dusty tarmac
    a boy on a swing

     head down
  mouth humming
a boy swinging intensely

    before dusk he must go
to his grandmother's house
    on the edge of the city

     alone on a swing
  thinking on a swing
     a boy

  his mother will stay home
   she won't go to the shelter
people here are afraid of shelters
   they remember last time

the chains of the swing
they clank they creak
the boy's head fills
   with explosions

   a boy on a swing

The Famous Battle

Dawn came creeping
On her soft grey paws

Dawn came creeping
On her soft grey paws

By the time the sun rose
She'd torn down the sky with her claws

The Norwegian Farmer

(In Peer Gynt, *the Pastor tells this story at the graveside)*

He wasn't rich and he wasn't clever.
His voice was quiet. He found words difficult.
He used to come into church as if somebody might hit him
And always, in public, he kept his right hand in his pocket.

When war broke out, we called up the young men.
They were weighed and measured – then they signed.
I sat beside the Captain.
The room was crowded with fathers.
Outside on the grass
The young men were fooling about and laughing.

Then this young man stepped forward,
White as the snow at the edge of a glacier.
'Come closer,' said the Captain, 'Closer.'
The young man rested his right hand on the table –
It was wrapped in bandages.
The young man mumbled something –
How his sickle had slipped by accident
And cut his finger off, by accident.

There was no sound at all in the room.
Then the Captain stood up.
He was as grey as steel.
And 'Get out,' the Captain said, 'Get out.'

So the young man got out, but it took a long time.
Fathers fell back on either side, and they stared and stared
As he walked the gauntlet between them
Until, eventually, he reached the door and ran
Out of the town up to his home in the mountains.

He leased a farm. He married. He built a house.
He broke up the hard ground. He managed well.
The small fields of his farm swayed with golden crops.

His first farm was destroyed by a flood.
He started again, created another farm.
His second farm was crushed by an avalanche.
He started again, his house rose again for the third time.

33

He and his wife had three sons, bright as buttons.
But their school was reached by a mountain path
Beside a terrifying ravine.
So the man tied himself to his eldest son,
And he carried the youngest son in his arms,
And he carried the other son on his back.
For years he struggled them through to school,
And they grew to be men, and they went to America,
And they became rich, and they forgot their father.

He was a short-sighted man.
He only talked to those who were close to him.
To him the rousing speeches of patriotic leaders
Had less meaning than the music of cowbells.
But he was humble, this old man with nine fingers was humble.
In the eyes of the state, he was a bad citizen perhaps,
But in the little country of his family –
There he was a great man. There he was himself.

So, peace be with you.
You fought bravely in the war all farmers fight.
I hope that today you stand before God
And He smiles as you take your right hand out of your pocket
And your right hand is whole again.

(based on a literal translation by Karin Bamborough)

The Last Goofs on Earth Say Sorry to Their Favourite Star

now we have done
what no one else has done

we have undone
the sun
our sun
it was the only one

the golden rays
of olden days
are gone gone gone

and here we sit
in a crevasse of black regret

from
unrise
to
unset

SHADOW SPEECHES

The Shadow Poet Laureate moves in a mysterious way, something like a dark starfish. Occasionally it behoves him to speak rather than spout in public. Finding it hard to ad lib without swearing or soppiness, he writes down his prophetic if pathetic thoughts and reads them out. These are sometimes mistaken for poems and people even ask for copies. The rest of the pieces in this section were written for public performance.

All the Light There Is was commissioned as a New Year 2003 poem for the BBC World Service – the Shadow recorded it and the BBC broadcast it all over the planet.

When They Tell You to Go to War was spoken at a meeting about Vietnam and Iraq and also in Hyde Park at the historic rally of February 15th, 2003. The Shadow was early on the bill and people had only been coming into the Park for an hour or so, but he was satisfied with an audience of around 250,000.

Work To Do was written on the brink of the 2003 invasion of Iraq and spoken in Grosvenor Square on my wife Celia's birthday. I'd been listening to a lot of speeches and some of them had seemed destructive to me. I wanted to speak up for the many pacifists in the anti-war movement.

Beating Your Head I had intended to read at the Poetry Society. But I was a guest and I felt it might sound personally rude.

So here it is...

All the Light There Is

We tossed a coin marked two thousand and three
Heads for Peace, Tails for War – which'll it be?

Came down Tails – and I heard a voice:
'Welcome to the Monster Zoo!
We're going to unlock all the cages
And save Democracy for you.

'And out will march monsters
whose work is war.
Their hearts are hot
as the planet's core.

'For power and money
they murder the poor,
then they rape each other
till war breeds war

'And the air cracks into shrapnel,
the oceans turn to lead
and the earth itself is burning
and all the light is dead.'

Yes the monsters are rattling their cages
their keepers are reaching for the keys
and some of us are cheering on the monsters,
and some of us are down on our knees

singing

     we love the light
all the light there is
   come and let's walk
into the light of peace

no more war   no more war

Yes – it was Heads for peace, and a newborn child
cuddled to its mother's breast.
Of all the visions I ever saw
this vision was the best.

So a New Year's born –
it gasps, it cries.
Gather up the baby –
gaze into its eyes

Sing to the baby
on the warm breast.
Let the child drink peace,
let the mother rest.

    singing

  we love the light
all the light there is
  love is the light
all the light there is
  peace is the light
all the light there is
  come and let's walk
into the light of peace

no more war   no more war

When They Tell You to Go to War

don't go
don't go to work
don't go to school
don't go to the movies
don't go to college
don't go to your regiment
don't go to your ship
don't go to your air base

go into the streets
take over the streets
and bring Britain to a full stop

when they tell you to go to war
don't go
don't go to war

Work to Do

I'm a pacifist.
If you're a pacifist too
You know that as soon as you say:
I'm a pacifist –
A Political Person smiles and says:
Of course I respect your position, but –

Well I say: I don't want your respect –
How about your help?
We've got work to do.
And the Political Person smiles and asks
The same stupid question time after time:
Wouldn't you have fought World War Two
To stop Hitler?
And I say: No – and here's the reason why.
Because I wouldn't have fought World War One –
So Hitler wouldn't have come to power.

Don't you understand
After all these centuries
That war gives birth to war
War gives birth to war?
That's how the murder plague grows
Unless we stop it.
Yes, we've got work to do.

Many of us feel weary.
We've been marching against the war
And talking against the war
And reading about the war
And watching the TV war
And we're tired of watching slaughter
And listening to the excuses for slaughter.

And in this time of grief
We often find ourselves on the brink of tears.
OK, let the tears flow.
Then wipe them away.
Have a party, get a good night's sleep –
And start again.
We've got work to do.

We put on the greatest demo
Ever seen in Britain.
We put on the greatest demo
Ever seen in wartime Britain.
That's a start.

But we've got to stop this war.
Stop the next war.
Stop all wars.

We find ourselves now
In the middle of World War Three –
The war which started
When nuclear bombs dropped
On Hiroshima and Nagasaki –
World War Three –
The war between the rich and the poor.
That's the task ahead of us –
To bring an end to World War Three.
To heal the wounds of the world.
To bring peace throughout the world.
We've got work to do.

We'll work with our French and German
and American and Russian and Chinese
and Pakistani and Cuban and South African
and Iraqi brothers and sisters.
We'll make the United Nations
A blessing on the world.
We'll teach our children and our grandchildren
That we have done enough killing,
That killing people is wrong.
With them, we'll examine pacifism
And ways of non-violent resistance
To cruel oppressors and benevolent oppressors.

We'll study and celebrate the lives
Of Gandhi and Martin Luther King
And their brave followers.
We'll set up Commissions of Truth and Reconciliation
All over the world – including Ireland.
We'll help to organise
The vast majority of the people of the planet
Who long for peace
And whose deepest wish
Is No More War.

And that's our work
No More War.

So, like my Jamaican comrade
Andrew Salkey used to say:
Brothers and sisters –
Keep on keeping on –
We've got work to do.

Beating Your Head

Would like to see a Poetry Society
which mobilised its membership
to campaign for our poets
to be paid wages rather than the odd hand-out
honoured here
as they are honoured in Ireland?

Would like to see a Poetry Society
which mobilised its membership
to campaign for all the media
to sit up and take notice and use poetry?

I had a vision of the future of poetry on radio
Poetry FM
A station with poetry of all the world
poetry of every age
new and old verse plays of every country

I've been trying to discuss this with
the heads of BBC radio, but when I mentioned it
at the Poetry Society in the hope of
encouragement I was told –

I'M AFRAID YOU'RE BEATING YOUR HEAD
AGAINST A BRICK WALL

Beating our heads
Against a brick wall
Beating our heads
Against a brick wall
That's how we make our music

Poets United
Beating our heads
Beating our heads
Against brick walls

How did Shakespeare
Build his golden theatre?
How did William Blake
Build Jerusalem?

How did Emily Dickinson
And John Keats
Build their beautiful follies?
Beating their heads
Beating their heads
Against a brick wall

What brought the slave trade tumbling down?
Who got rid of hanging in England?
What stopped the Poll Tax and the Tories?
How can we stop the war against Iraq
This war they call inevitable?

People United
Beating our heads
Beating our heads
Against a brick wall

Keep beating your head
And when it starts bleeding
Use the blood to write
More poems on the wall
Saying come and join us
Come and beat your head
Against this bloody wall
And soon you'll see
The wall begin to shake
And the first bricks begin to fall

ENGLANDING

Englanding

We are the cold-eyed English
from the islands of the rain
and our cold eyes are not looking at you
so how can you say we are cold to you
when you are less than nothing at all to us
and we save the cold of our eyes
for the eyes of our cold families
on the islands of the rain

We are the cold-eyed English
and at six in the evening we raise our glasses
our glasses of luke-warm sherry
and we say cheers and here's to you
to the Manager of the Bank of Cold
and the Vicar of the Church of Cold
and the Teacher who teaches our children Cold
at the School of Coldness, which gets results
and which we can just afford
thanks to grandma's shares
in the Iceberg which sank the Titanic.

New Year

when your head feels like a rotting potato
and your dreams are all mixed up with your thoughts
because you drift in and out of sleep
in jerks like a raft on a complicated river
of oxbow bends and rapids and backwater sludge
with a dozen daffodils every ten paces along the bank
how much a bunch? come on I haven't got all day!
and you shake yourself awake and stare out of the window
and there is the sky like a rotting potato

there are little pains like bent paperclips
in every portion of your body
and your stomach is like a city on fire
and your brain is like a stomach full of wind

and you open your hand
and look into your palm
and there you see your life
what's left of it

maybe it looks like a marble
with miniature whirling clouds inside
among flecks of gold

maybe it looks like an albino rhinoceros
trudging towards the Mountains of Amnesia

maybe it looks like that fucking potato
so you tear it apart
and it's not so much a matter of rotting potato
as blue bruises and rotten growths
and transparent worms and stinking spudge

you don't have to be psychic to feel the jab

not much left of your life
and the hardest part to go
with the heart's battery weak
and the logic clock running amok

not much left of your life
and all those easy little things –
the tying of a shoelace

the writing of a letter
the walk along the street
where it always rains or seems to be raining
the forming of a smile –
all seem as difficult
as eating galvanised buckets.

and so in a mashed sort of way
you begin to consider suicide
just to put a stop to all this stupid stuff
and maybe you can work out a way
which won't hurt you, not much,
but every time you focus clearly enough
to calculate that fatal cocktail
you realise It'll Hurt Us More Than It Hurts You
as the angel choir of those you love
sings in your waxy ears

The Strangers

In most countries of the world, from ancient times, there is a customary way of meeting strangers – recorded by Homer among others. It's the way I have been met in poor countries – in South African and Chilean shanty towns – with warmth and generous hospitality.

You are supposed to greet the stranger and offer them whatever they need. You sit down with them and eat and drink with them. You talk with them and give them a safe place to sleep. Only when they are fed and rested do you have the right to ask their name or where they come from. Coldness or hostility to strangers is very unlucky. The stranger might be your long-lost father, your daughter, an angel or a god.

From the child-murderer Poverty
Or the claws of the Nightmare Police,
Painfully over land and sea
They come seeking some kind of peace,

They travel to our green and golden lands
Hoping to build lives that are free and good.
Let's take our brothers' and our sisters' hands
And make them welcome, as a family should.

National Pride Haiku

  if smacking children
 were an Olympic event
England would take gold

O Mrs Simpson!

Guy Marcus Trundle
Son of a Vicar from York
A bit of a dancer one hell of a chancer
Who knew how to roast your pork

Guy Marcus Trundle
A man from the motor trade
You climbed on board his tailor-made Ford
And he drove you to Biggleswade

O Mrs Simpson
That leather upholstery smell!
You'd been on the top of Von Ribbentropp
But he never changed gear so well

As Guy Marcus Trundle
With a hamper packed in the boot
Guy Marcus Trundle
In his double-breasted suit

'Oh tilt your trilby and bundle me up
Fondle and fumble me
Then trundle me home to the Prince of Wales
In time for our afternoon tea.'

Fun in World War Two

Get your mack out
Call Uncle Jack out
To enjoy the black-out

We'll go to Piccadilly Circus
And feel up the workers
Maybe one of them will jerk us

Ode to the Tellytubbies

the golfcourse in Hell
the Trident periscope
and the Four Fucking Foetuses

Douglas

Douglas is seventy. He wears striped pyjamas.
Faded blue and murky white-striped pyjamas
As he pads barefoot across the frosted backyard
Carrying a bucket of cinders and ashes.
Oh Douglas such a hero such a fool to yourself
Hair sticking up like an old white dandelion.

The backyard poster glows with golden coinage –
Gold To Have And To Hold oh the gold looks good enough to eat with a spoon.
Does a jackpot trapdoor open in the floor of Heaven
To goldenfall down a shower of gold Britannias?
It does not. Not for Douglas.
He empties his bucket and all it holds now is the cold.

School for ten years.
Work for forty years.
Pension for five years so far
And not much further.
We have finished with Douglas now
For this is England and it is wintertime and it is eat or be eaten.

Banned for Six Months

My Jaguar is mine and I am hers.
She's my Madonna. Say a prayer –
Orphans, widows, widowers.

I touch a switch. My wild witch purrs:
'I'll take you anyshiningwhere.'
My Jaguar is mine and I am hers.

Give her the gun and Wiltshire blurs.
Two cyclists. Wham! A hedgehog. Squash! A hare –
Orphans, widows, widowers.

Why don't they vivisect child-murderers?
Pass me the in-car vodka. Yeah.
My Jaguar is mine and I am hers.

We're off beyond speedometers
Into a ghostly fog. Who's there?
Orphans, widows, widowers.

The Court. Their family – the whimperers.
My firm fixes a driver. I don't care –
My Jaguar is mine and I am hers,
Orphans, widows, widowers.

Ice-rink Participation

clapalong crapalong
stolidly skittish
on the beat off the beat
out of time british

The Dudley Lightbulb Story

Have you seen Mr Dudley Lightbulb
padding over the lawn of the Eventide Home
in his convict pyjamas and berserk haircut?

off to lurk in the ruined stables?
off to work in his Secret Electronomous Laboratory!

every morning
such a blowing of glass
such a fiddling of wires
such a squeezing of gas

every lunchtime he invents the lightbulb

every lunchtime
such fizzy lemonade illumination
such fizzy hearted excitement
such fizzy-oh-therapeutical celebration

and what shall he name his invention?
it is so bald and brilliant
he decides to name it after himself

somewhere between the cheese salad and the grey pudding
the inmate on his left hand side asks:
how many Lightbulbs will it take
to screw in a lightbulb?
the inmate on his right hand side says:
if you're naming it after yourself
why not call it Dud Lightbulb?
the razzle-dazzle brightitude in his brain
fades to a dark spot like a switched off TV set

every lunchtime he invents the lightbulb
every evening he forgets he done it

have you seen Mr Dudley Lightbulb
padding down the corridor to his room
in his gravy jacket and his sheepdog slippers?

silly is as silly does, no doubt –
but are you half as happy as Mr Dudley Lightbulb?

To Somebody Considering Suicide

        up to you
we'd sooner you didn't
but it's up to you

        your mind
    your body
        your life
    your heart
they're all yours
and it's up to you

if you throw them all away
we'll be sorry and sad
and we'll wave goodbye
and now and then cry
but we won't throw our own lives away
we'll stick around down here
and whenever we can
we'll have a good time

        if you've got the guts
there are hundreds of other moves
you could make or try to make
instead of that one move
        you can't take back

imagine other choices
imagine those changes of
        places
        people
        jobs
missions or visions
all those other paths

but if every path leads you
    to the same brick wall
        it's up to you
        bang your head
        on the wall
    till you're dead
        or stop
take a good look at the wall

55

what's stuck on it?
a stupid poster advertising dread?
        tear it off
        underneath
may be graffiti by Bessie Smith
may be a phoenix by Turner

        and maybe
fingerholds and toeholds
    between the bricks
    so haul yourself up
    and climb that wall
        climb up and over
        that fucking wall

        but it's
        up to you
if you can't make it
        sorry
very sorry but we won't
carry your bones around with us
        everywhere
we've got dances to try
and other chips to fry
        before we lie
        down and let
            the wall
        fall on us

        meanwhile
whatever you choose to do
        up to you,
            love,
        up to you.

for mental patients

    pull yourself together
that's what they always say
    pull yourself together
  throw your cares away
    pull yourself together
but if they knew my heart
and how it kicks inside me
      they'd say
   pull yourself apart

    all together now

Doctor Rat Explains

we place each subject
in a complicated maze
with high walls and bright-flickering lights

to those who work well –
pressing down the correct levers –
we give rewards

to those who prove useless –
recalcitrant, scratching themselves in corners –
we allot punishments

the rewards
are the gourmet delights of Wealth

the punishments
are the electric aches and pains of Poverty

this experiment proves
that the meaning of Money can be taught
to the majority of human beings

Asteroid

an asteroid the size of a football pitch
a football pitch a football pitch
hurtled by only seventy-five thousand miles from Earth
and in astronomical circles that a near-miss
a near-miss yes

if it had hit the Earth
which it didn't do
by only seventy-five thousand miles
it would have exploded with the power
of twenty thousand Hiroshima bombs
twenty thousand twenty thousand

scientists only spotted the asteroid
the asteroid the asteroid
they only spotted the asteroid
three days after it passed the Earth

good work chaps
you photographed its arse

what was name of the asteroid
the one the size of a football pitch
what was the name of the asteroid
that missed us by only seventy-five thousand miles

well it's surface was smooth and firm and green
smooth and firm and green
and it was being marked out
by whitewash line machines
pushed by two teenagers
called Denzel and Pug

but what was the name of the asteroid
the one the size of a football pitch
what was the name of the asteroid
        it was called Anfield

The Sleeping King

Slumped at a marble table
Through which his beard has grown,
For centuries the King has slept
Upon his radium throne.

The page boy standing guard nearby
Hears the blurred words which seep
Between the lips of the old King
Murmuring in his sleep:

'Boy, run to the Tower of London –
See if the ravens appear,
For if they do, I must slumber on
For another hundred year.

'Boy, swim to the Rock of Gibraltar –
Observe if the apes be there,
For, while they occupy that Rock,
I must sleep in my radium chair.

'But, should that Rock be monkeyless
And raven-bereft the Tower
I'll arise from my royal slumbers
And reassume my power

'And the flames of England's glory
And of her imperial might
Shall spread around the globe once more
To banish barbarous night.'

The page boy listens to these words,
So poignantly prophetic,
Fills the syringe and gives the King
His daily anaesthetic.

(after *The Sleeping Emperor* by Friedrich Ruckert, 1815)

In a Brown Paper Bag

in a brown paper bag
is a crown of gold
in the crown of gold
is a loaf of bread
in the loaf of bread
is a loaded pistol

take out the gold crown
put it on your head
order your brother
to give you the bread
it's fifty-fifty
he'll shoot you instead

Artefactions

Misery Me!

(This is a song from my stage version of *The Lion, The Witch and The Wardrobe*.
It is sung by Lucy, a young evacuee who has been sent with her brothers and sisters
to the country during the bombing of London in World War Two. There she has
discovered a wardrobe through which she can reach the magical land of Narnia.
But nobody believes her. All she can do is sing her heart out to the audience.)

When Alice came home from Wonderland
Did her family laugh and jeer?
When Crusoe sailed back from his island
Did they say: You imagined it dear?
When Dorothy flew in her ruby slippers
From the Emerald City of Oz
Did her Auntie Em say it was all a dream?
I bet they all did, because –

    Father's in the Royal Navy
    Somewhere out at sea
    I'm dreaming of submarines –
        Misery me!
    Mother would come down from London
    But she isn't free
    I'm dreaming of falling bombs –
        Misery me!

We're here in the heart of the country
And we dive in the pond by the mill
And we fish for trout in the river
And we slide down the side
Of a bumpy old hill
And I should be as happy as Larry
Playing Cowboys and Indians all day
But everyone believes I'm a liar
So I wish I could grow some wings
And fly far away

    Father's in the Royal Navy
    Somewhere out at sea
    I'm dreaming of Narnia –
        Misery me!
    Mother would come down from London
    But she isn't free
    I'm dreaming of Narnia –
        Misery me!

Music
(from *Orpheus Sings*)

Tough little grass
Growing with the heather
Where the ancient mountains dream
And out of the grass
A spring begins to bubble
And overflows into a stream

Stony foot stream
Slithers down the hillside
Races past an old stone wall
It laughs at the sheep
And dashes by the shepherd
To dive into the waterfall

Waterfall flood
Boiling in the rockpool
Spouting down with all its force
It whirls and it swells
And dodges round the boulders
To join the river's shining course

River of light
Joining other rivers
Wandering so powerfully
The farms and the towns
Are nourished by its waters
Until it meets the golden sea

And music is the spring
And music is the stream
Music is the waterfall
Music is the river
And music is the golden sea
Of the soul
Music is the golden sea

The Most Requested Poem on the Radio Programme
Poetry If You Don't Mind Awfully

Gosh, yes I remember Addlestrop –
A poetry reviewer in the days of Bop.
His prose was like flat ginger pop.
He lived like a ghost and he died like a mop –
That's all I recall of old Addlestrop

Max Ernst Prophesies

Europe After the Rain –

    a relief map
of a boot-trampled continent

the Mediterranean
pulled out of shape
like some exhausted
pale blue ghost

shipping routes
are dotted lines
criss–crossing
the dry water

the borders of nations
marked black and straight

but there are no ships
there are no soldiers

    and these words float into my head:

they are playing with the death of the planet

Coincidence

In three days in Paris
   I saw five people
who looked just like
   Mark Lawson

   Mark Lawson
lives in London
where he does the work
   of fifteen journalists

     back in London
I switched on the telly
and running down a street in Pakistan
I saw five thousand demonstrators
   who looked exactly like
     Melvyn Bragg

At the Reichenbach Falls

(for Liz, Mark, Angie, Marcus, J.J. and Izzy, May 1998)

one white star
on the rock
marks the spot
on the cliff
path
where
Holmes
and
Moriarty
rocked
back and forth
before
they fell
clutching
each other
at last
into the swirling white
petticoat
of the waterfall's lap

what did they cry to each other
as they fell?
master
detective
master
criminal
hurled
together
in a
violent
mating
flesh into flesh
bone into bone
bodies on stone
and
breaking
what did they cry to each other
locked in each other's arms?

Left Bank Poem

You
Can use the loo
As soon as I'm through
À La Recherche Du Temps Perdu.

Literary Tip Number 317

Don't read Sylvia Plath
While shaving in the bath.

A Sense of Complicity: *Advertising Supplement*

William Sieghart likes poetry. He sponsors poetry competitions which help some poets, even if many of us don't much like poetry beauty contests.

But the day after May Day this year, William sent me 'a rare poetry commission opportunity. A leading advertising agency would like to use poetry in a forthcoming advertising campaign for one of its clients. As a result, I am helping them commission poems from poets.' Each poet will be paid £200. Up to £3,000 will be paid to authors of the 24 poems used in TV and radio adverts.

What sort of poems? Well, the adverts are aimed at the 45-60 age group. 'They are adverts, so although very different from normal commercial break fodder the poetry needs to be relatively upbeat, conversational, witty and thought-provoking. The main criterion is that the poems should give a sense of complicity and should make the listener feel understood.' And so on.

Why does this matter a damn? Because poetry is one of the few places in our civilisation where you can expect to be told the truth. And advertising is (very well paid) prostitution. So I wrote to William:

Advertising Will Eat the World

> art is the desperate search
> for truth and beauty
> a matter of life and death
>
> advertising is the cynical hunt
> for maximum profit
> a matter of lies for money
>
> poetry makes love with the language
> advertising rapes the language

music dances with children and gives them wings
advertising steals from children and artlsts
art is the opposite of advertising

> poetry just ran to me
> she is weeping on my shoulder
It hurts her to be in the same poem as advertising
> 'Get rid of them,' she whispers to me,
> 'Send those fucking advertisers away.'

yours sincerely,
Adrian Mitchell, Shadow Poet Laureate

PS: I hope no poets collaborate with your mistaken scheme.

NOTE: I also enclosed the following two advertising poems, but William never replied to me, so I published the lot in *Red Pepper*. William still doesn't write.

Rest in Peace, Andy Warhol. Enjoy.

Elvis and Jackie Onassis
Marilyn and Mao-tse Tung –
They all looked alike to you

You sucked out their veins
Now all that remains
Is a series of lifeless adverts for you

Shallow as a shiny puddle
You were proud of your shallowness.

You started as an advertising man.
You ended as an advertising man.
And you sold your product – Selfishness.

Relax, Andy, you weren't the first.
And you certainly weren't the worst.
Necrophilia got much sillier –
Step forward Damien Hirst.

Pioneers, O Pioneers!

Guns before Butter!
Strength through joy!
   Knock-out slogans.

SS lightning bolts!
Swastika armbands!
   Stunning logos.

Hitler and Goebbels!
   Brilliant admen.

LAKESIDE

Snapshots taken from the audience at a poetry reading beside the lake in the Piedras Blancas Ecological Park, Comenfalco, Colombia, June 3rd 2001
(with thanks to the Medellin International Poetry Festival and to the British Council)

To K. Michel (Holland)

you sit sideways
fingers locked
as something like your poem is read in Spanish
beside a small Colombian lake

behind your head
a mirror image
of cloudy green woods
and the underwater yellow
of genuine sand

there is so much fakery in this world
but this feels oddly like real life

your turn now
in your own Dutch voice
whatever it is
sounds clear and true

you finish your poem
put it down gently
and flinch away from
a sky-diving Colombian bee

Bei Dao Reads His Poems (China)

both hands full
of multi-coloured pebbles

he pours them carefully
in ones and twos
and fives and sixes
on to the rain-drenched grass
for us to look at

wondering

On the Lake

the ghosts of ferns and conifers
relaxing on the surface of the take

a sudden panic
as a blue boy throws in a stick
to be retrieved by his imaginary dog

For Hayat Saif (Bangladesh)

as a rose-red lump
of clay revolves
upon the potter's wheel

his words revolve
and take their form
from the strong fingers of his voice

a tall and perfect vase
arises
colour of the rose-red earth

Digressions

the tall lean dark poet
   reads sensibly
though his hands are shaking

      but he's upstaged
   by a stretched elastic and ecstatic
            waterbird

and by the drunken stagger
   of a woolly toddler
   clutching her bottle

      OK says the toddler
   welcome to normality

      fly on, waterbird.
      keep reading, poet,

I'll go on exploring a world
   still wet behind the ears

As the Lakeside Poetry Reading Ends

      small rain
      spells out
   its starry-coded messages
      across the water

Just Doing My Job

I stride down to the edge of the lake.
Has it been lurking in this innocent-looking valley
For ten thousand years or seven months?
I ask it sternly:
What are you doing here?
I'm from the Water Police.

Intergalactic Poetry Festival

And, for our ten thousand and forty-ninth poet tonight
I'm glad to introduce
Gugrug the Blarm 76% Thermox
    from the Shooooosh Galaxy.

A ganglion-shaped being
    is floated on to the stage
        and begins its programme of
            Thought Ray Versicles

ZOV ZOV   ZOV–ZOV
    ZOOOOOOOOOOV!
        voz

The ten thousand and forty-eight poets
    who have already performed
appear to listen wisely despite the lack of a translation
    then applaud gently
with hands, fins, tentacles, lobes and chromosomes

La Chiba

*(My first poem in Spanish written after taking a ride down a mountainside
in an open–sided Colombian bus (or* chiba*) full of people and wild music.)*

            ABAJO!
            ARRIBA!
        VIVA LA CHIBA!

    (Down!
    Up!
Long Live the Bus!)

Chiba Ride

Silver horse leaps on the prow of the chiba
groaning as it hauls up the side of the mountain
past the shot-up yellow diamond road-signs

Seven Ages of Screen Woman

Now the world is a Hollywood movie
All the women are movie stars
Riding around in four-wheel-drives
Drinking in health juice bars

At ninety she plays a wise old girl
With laughter in her eyes and such
Don't matter if she kind of slurs her lines
Cos nobody's listening much
At the Oscars she looks as good as new
Thanks to her surgeon's skill
And when it's time for her final scene
She'll just – pop a little pill

The sixty-year-old actress
Plays a glamorous chanteuse who
Is making her Broadway comeback
At the age of forty-two
But a starlet discovers her secret
And threatens to expose her shame
But our heroine wins a Tony
In the 17th revival of *Mame*

She's a doctor or explorer at forty
Acting sassy but ultra-brave
She battles medical corruption
Or fights Nazis in a Pharaoh's grave
Eighty minutes into the movie
She's struggling for survival
Just hang on kid for our gal will end
Married to her patient or her handsome rival

At twenty–five she's a teacher
On a stagecoach travelling West
She's warned not to stop in Bashville
By a sheriff in a dirty old vest
A former gunslinger saves her
When the Skull Gang torch her school
He's twice her age and half her brain
But she goes and marries the fool

At eighteen she's a virgin
In love with a Basketball Champ
They attend a rockroll High School
Where the teachers are all crazy or camp
The storyline's about as dumb as they come
But it's better than her last script
When she played a screaming kid being hunted down
By the Slasher of the Crypt

At nine she's cast as the youngest
Of a Mid-West family who
Relate to each other from day to night
And share all their problems too
The town get flooded, kid wakes up
To save Granny, who's an invalid
And the President gives her a medal
And everybody hugs the kid

The baby actress is more of a prop
Just a plump little bundle of dreams
Being passed from actor to actor
(We can edit out her screams)
She wishes she could stay in her cool little cot
Instead of in the blinding light
But her chaperone is drinking quite nearby
So everything will be all right

And one day she'll play a very old lady
Who's in love with a younger man
And she'll certainly win an Oscar
For that's the Almighty Plan
For the world is a Hollywood movie
All the women are movie stars
Riding around in four-wheel-drives
And drinking in health juice bars

And if that's not the way you see it
Better change the way you see
It may not be the way you want it
But that's the way it's gonna be

Shou Lao, God of Longevity

The Garden at the South Pole
Shines silver in the sun
Round and round the peach tree
The red-faced children run

Their Grandfather, astride a Crane
Flies down and perches in the tree
He plucks and drops down to each child
A peach of Immortality

The Café Kafka

A curving corridor
of vanilla pillars
and pistachio plasterwork.
It's an edible café,
the Café Kafka.

Lampglobes bulge
and overflow
with splashing light.
Even the draughts which flow
along the diamond-patterned floor
are warm in the Café Kafka.

Outside the Café Kafka
the third snow of winter
is slinking through Helsinki
and my charcoal fedora sits proudly
on the black marble table-top.

Only six hours ago,
when I met her
in her magical studio,
her first words were:
'What a beautiful hat!'
Who said that about my hat?
The mother of the Moomins,
Tove Jansson.

The Tourist Guide at Malmo Town Hall

Our Poetry Festival
has had such an effect
that we even have horses to read
and even write poetry

I read poetry
I do then fall down
and have some other views

Oscar the Second of Sweden

This is a ten-foot portrait
of Oscar the Second
He was called the Poet King
and wrote whenever the Muse beckoned
He only signed his published poems
with the single letter O
but they were so gruesomely written
that everyone did know
they must be the verses
of Oscar the Second
Who was called the Poet King

At the International Poetry Conference

twenty-five international poets
are driven in a minibus
to see the sights of Sweden

five unknown languages
whirl around my head
as the poets
answer their mobiles

I'm on the chariot, they cry –
Que pasa?

On the Stone Ship

On the grassy deck
of the great stone ship
   sit the stone sailors
drinking salt from granite bottles
   singing in voices of gravel:

   watch the stone eggs
watch out they are hatching
in every country of the world
watch the stone eggs of Hitler

   What shall we do
with the stone eggs of Hitler?
Send them to heaven
in stone spaceships?
Send them to hell
in submarines of stone?

   No – grind them up
into silvery sandy beaches
for our multi-coloured grandchildren
and our multi-coloured dogs

'Michael' by William Wordsworth

This poem by William Wordsworth
is often taught in schools.

It starts off with one and a half pages
saying how the story which follows
has no startling incidents
nothing much exciting about it
in fact two hundred per cent boring
but guaranteed suitable
for the fireside
for the fire more like
well Wordsworth was a Carlisle supporter

Of course poetry's important to the revolution.
Why else would they spend so much time in schools
teaching you to hate it?

This poem by William Wordworth
is often taught in schools
often taught in schools
often taught in schools

(It is important to go to school
in order to learn
how to be more like William Wordsworth.)

Variation

peaceful waters of the air
under an echo's branches

peaceful waters of a pool
under a bough laden with stars

peaceful waters of your mouth
under a forest of kisses

(from Federico García Lorca's poem 'Variacion')

What Poetry Says

(a free translation from Remco Campert)

Poetry says: Yes, I'm alive.
Poetry says: No., I'm not alone.

Poetry is the day after tomorrow
Dreaming of Wednesday week
In a far country, with you, aged 89 and a half.

Poetry breathes in and out,
It puts the beat in my feet,
It makes them hesitate and hover
Over the earth which longs for them to dance on it.

Voltaire got smallpox, but he cured himself
By swigging 200 pints of lemonade
Etcetera. That's poetry, man.

And look at the ocean, look at the surf.
It breaks on the rocks.
It breaks and breaks but – it's never broken.
Up it jumps again – that's poetry

Every word that anyone writes
Is an attack on old age.
You want a safe bet?
Put your money on death.

And what is death? Only the hush in the hallway
After the last words have been spoken.

Death, death, death –
It's an emotion.
It moves.

Asia Dream Poem

Clearings among the South-east Asian jungle
Spacious wooden octagonal huts
Built on wooden platforms
With high-up woven-leaf ceilings.
Three beds.
Bedside chests of drawers.
On mine – some photos,
Washing things, a cardboard page
Bearing a Kipling poem.
Three beds.
A man in each of the other beds.
All three of us lying silently,
Afraid to speak.
Lying under rough army blankets.

We knew
Our guards were all around outside
Waiting
Maybe they were eating and drinking
Getting ready.
They were going to set fire to the huts
And burn us in the huts.
Anyone who tried to run away
Would be hacked down to their knees with swords
And tortured to death.

It seemed better to lie silently in bed
And wait to burn.
I was lying there
Thinking, in detail, about being burned to death.
Some water had dripped on to the Kipling poem.
I wiped it dry.
The quicker everything burned the better.
I thought of taking off my watch.
My wrist might burn quicker.
At least I would not, while I was burning,
Have the pain of a guard grabbing
And tearing its metal strap
From my smouldering wrist.
I decided to leave it on,
just in case there might be any hope.

There seemed to be no hope.

I thought about my hair burning.
I tried to block out
Any further thought of burning.
I thought of my feet.
In case of hope
I should grab not my sandals
But my thickest boots
For the running across
The red-hot grass.
I thought of the others –
How still and silent.
I tried to think of a way
Of making myself unconscious.

There was a sound outside,
Around our hut.
The sound of liquid splashing on to the ground.
Pouring generously.
Probably petrol.

But then – huge sounds and blazes.
I had to sit up to look
Even though to sit up might be
To invite a bayonet.
And – looking out –
Flashes and roaring from the black sky
Great cones of blazing huts
And a kind of music
Made up of shouts and cheering.

Into our hut strode this big woman
The spitting image of Gracie Fields
'Follow me,' she said,
'We're getting out of here.'
And we leapt to our feet
But the scene changed
Before she could strike up *Sing As We Go…*

And there was Susan Sontag
Showing me her opera libretto
About our near burning,
But technically her verse was very awkward.
There was a couplet something like:

   We did not want to burn, each
   Of us felt that, on that beach.

We just need a couple of verses here, I said.
Let's keep it very simple.
I began to work on it.
My first line was:
I was not born to burn...

What happened to the scene
About our escape?
Had our guards fled from the bombing?
Did they come back after the raid?

I woke up and flung out my hand
And spilled part of a glass tankard of water
Over the diary and invitations
On my bedside table.
I put on the light to dry them with
A roll of kitchen paper.

I lay there for five ten minutes
Thinking I'll forget this
No I'll remember this
No I won't
I'll get up and write it down.
I did.

In all that dream
I never saw one of the guards
But I can still feel
The fear of the fire.
We were not born to burn.

Blake on His Childhood Visions

The first time I saw God
Was when I was four years old.
He put his head in the window
And set me a-screaming.

When I was about eight
I was walking on Peckham Rye
When I looked up into a tree
And it was full of angels –
Their bright wings
Bespangling every bough like stars.
I ran home to tell my parents.
Mother had to stop my father beating me for lying.

Everyone has the gift of seeing visions, yes.
But they lose it, because they don't work at it.

King Lear's Fool Waves Goodbye

here I go
holding on to sanity
in one hand
like a bottle of green and stagnant
mineral water

here I go
holding on to nonsense
in the other hand
like a mobile phone
made of marzipan

I take a swig of pond:
Hello, I'm on the surface
of some sort of planet
or peanut

holding on
brothers and sisters
holding on

AUTOMAGIC

Memoirs

let ghosts imagine
    being alive
I well remember
    being dead

Her Life
(another for my mother)

She didn't know the value of money –
it filtered in her purse and flooded out.

She didn't know the value of the body –
something she shrugged about.

She didn't know the value of the love
which she transmitted ceaselessly.

She tried to hoist the wounded world on her frail shoulders –
It seemed a possibility.

Disguise

Every morning after I shampoo my fur
I climb into my humanskin costume and
Put on my human mask and human clothes.

Then I go out into the human city
And catch a human bus to work.

As I sit at my computer
Summoning up images of the financial world
None of my colleagues knows
That inside my human hand gloves
Are the brown and burly
Sharp and curly
Paws of a grizzly bear.

Yes, I am a bear in a cunning disguise,
Only passing as human
Trying not to yield to temptation
As I lumber past
The sticky buns in the baker's shop
The honeycombs in the health shop

I am married to a human woman who knows my secret
We have a human daughter
Who is rather furry and has deep golden eyes
And gentle paws
We call her Bruinhilda

I took Bruinhilda to a circus once
But there was a performing bear
Riding a unicycle, juggling with flames
Dancing to an accordion

I sat tight
Though she might have been my mother
I sat tight
While the inside of my human mask
Filled up with the tears of a bear

Dreaming Joan of Arc

I was bustling around an old French city square
Arranging desks in a circle on the cobbles
Placing computers on top of the desks
Trying to construct a kind of hedge of plastic
To make it harder for the gogglers to watch
     Joan in her agony.

I walked towards her. She stood in silk.
She stood in chains.
Her face was the face of a child, my child.
Fifteen pink roses jumped out of the ground
So I lifted them to her, placed them in her arms.
She cradled the roses and smiled and said: 'Why?'
I said: 'Because I love you with my body and my soul.
You are a good child.
Now you must sleep like a good child.'
And I knew the flames would start any second
And I said: 'Happy dreams'.
And I kissed her mouth twice.
Her mouth was a rose.

She was a child, she was a child
Like all the rest of us.

Suddenly I was with some university people
In something like a revolving door
And I was telling them about my dream
And how I'd been bustling around an old French city square –
But they kept interrupting me, and I don't blame them –
Being told someone else's dream is bad enough,
But when you're a character in someone else's dream
And they start telling you about the other dreams they're having –
That's worse than throwing ketchup over waiters.

I woke on a battered old planet
Where I have been put
With my five children and seven grandchildren,
A world where people are burned to death
By other people.

Fifteen pink roses
Their petals turning black
And curling back
     Joan

Grassy Cliffs

           grassy cliffs
        that I have dreamed
           grassy cliffs
        that I have dreamed
            so often
        and walked so often
        barefoot to the edge
and spread my arms wide wide
            and flown

My Crabby Apple Day

I was asked to write a Apple Poem –
Then I slipped and fell downstairs
And my bum looks like a Golden Delicious
Since it bumped down them apples and pears.
Now I know what a Granny Smith's feelings must be
When she falls off of her good old tree.

(after a tumble down the Pam Ayres,
September 19th, 2002 – written at the request
of Jeff Cloves for the Stroud Apple Festival)

First Publication

My poems were first published
on lavatory walls
down in the Gents
where the girl I loved could never see them
of course I didn't use her name
or sign the poems

Sometimes people smudged my words out
with piss or shit or snot
I didn't mind the piss so much
and the smudged poems
looked sort of streamlined and alive
when their blue letters became
soft streaks across the pockmarked yellow plaster

Hitler Dream

I am Norwegian.
So is my wife.
We have one daughter of twenty.
We have been planning
How to assassinate Hitler.

Suddenly the three of us are standing
In a narrow office
Outside Hitler's office.

Hitler and a large Gestapo officer
Walk in and look at us.
Hitler's dark ray stare
Fixes on each of us in turn.
We almost die of terror.

Hitler and the Gestapo man
Go back into Hitler's office for a second.
Then Hitler looks round the doorway and says:
We will see the daughter first.
He vanishes.
The Gestapo man takes our daughter into Hitler's office.

The door is open between the two offices
For a long moment.
I look at the window of the narrow office
Hoping we might jump out to our deaths
Or I might push my wife out just in time.

But the window is so closely barred
You couldn't stick your hand out
Between the bars, let alone your head.

I can feel the agony in my wife's heart
As the door between the offices closes.

Transblucency

a paper man
and a paper woman
rocked in their paper bed

the love they made
was poetry
with jazzbirds
gliding
overhead

Don't Answer It

Telephone rings but I let it ride
I don't want to know who's just died
I just move a little closer to my fireside
    and squeeze my eyes like lemons

Sometimes I feel like the nose of a mouse
Twitching like Groucho's highbrow eyebrows
Sometimes I feel like a slaughterhouse
    waiting for the next consignment

The flu bug hit me like the US Air Force
With ropes of phlegm it strangled me hoarse
And left me whispering Worcester sauce
    for poems of bubble and squeak

Sorry

Sure, I worked as a slave to Time
And knew his bullwhip's vicious touch
But didn't know who punished me
Or why my shoulders hurt so much

He rode me like a motorbike
On some mad ride through towns in flames.
My mind and body tensed with overwork
Till I could hardly say my children's names

And, maddened by his rhythmic lash,
Sometimes struck out at those I met
And hurt the innocent and weak –
I am still scarred by that regret.

Thanks to My Dog in an Hour of Pain

weariness
blankness in my bones
tears like molten lead shoulders down my throat
a dead white pebble
in the left side of my chest an empty fur glove where my heart
should be sitting
the clock strikes and won't stop striking
striking the time of grief
weariness
blankness in the bone

don't tell me I'm wrong I know I'm wrong
My Adam's apple like a knotted up wrongness
I should be dancing in muddy boots
but I find myself addressing this Deathbed Congress

and I say:
melodies carved down to the bone
fears like a stock exchange movie in a foreign language
I power-steer my pony down the off-side of a canyon
me and my dog have come to clean up this anguish

oh the dust bites and keeps on biting won't stop biting

        but
  sweet dog in the moon
  sweet dog in the snow
  sweet dog in the wheat
  sweet dog in my sweat
  in my mind in my heart
  and in my arms
  sweet dog how you save my life

for you see how bleak I am
  how blank I am
you view my collapse with love and no surprise
dear goldenface and deep down toffee eyes

Out of the Corner of My Eye Vision

Out of the corner of my left eye
I saw an owl no bigger than my thumbnail
perched on the dark between two paving-stones
in Croftdown Road, London NW5
as I was walking home with my golden retriever

I saw an owl no bigger than my thumbnail
but only for a sidelong passing glance
I didn't break my stride to pause and crouch
and lower my bulldozer hands
to shunt that bird into a cage of tissues
to be borne home to the table mountain
of our kitchen table
for the bewonderment of our elephant cat
to photograph the mini-owl
to phone the newspapers
and the Royal Society for the Protection of Birds

No, I left the owl to its own tiny devices
its own micro-mice and squirrels
its own life its own universe
where owls no bigger than a human thumbnail
emerge from the dark between two paving-stones
inhale the petrolled air and dive back down again
through the dark between the paving-stones
to wherever owls no bigger than a thumbnail live

And so the newspapers, and the TV
And the two serious men in suits
with a third man taking notes
and the street cordoned off
with trembling fluorescent plastic strips
and the soldiers in germ-resistant white overalls
and glassy helmets
stubby guns cradled in their arms
and a couple of tanks at the end of each street
and JCBs and overgrown Tonka Toys
have not arrived to observe and guard and excavate
the dark between the paving-stones
into a gaping pit, a chasm
with special forces abseiling down the chasm
overseen by bristling helicopters

98

as they flicker down down down and out of sight
into that other universe
where owls are no bigger than a human thumbnail
but germs, perhaps, are a thousand times the size
of the knee-cap of God

Pour Soul

My body was a pleasant house
bit of a responsibility
what with a leaky roof frozen pipes
that burglary a touch of dry rot
and the legendary subsidence
but it mildly pleased me
as I strolled from room to room
or curled up on the window-seat
to watch the ebb and flow of the street

But one night I dreamed the dream of death
and woke up in the ashes of my house
a homeless soul
two dark eyes
a towelling dressing gown
and two blue feet
that's what I felt like
a soul without a home

The cold street wind ruffled my mind
and loneliness ran through my veins
I floated to my wife's house and rang the doorbell
but my fingers were made of mist
and the button wouldn't press
when I knocked the door with all my might
my knuckles produced only a flimsy hiss
and when I breathed on the window
the glass did not even reflect my face

Of course I tried other houses –
my children, my best friends –
houses bursting with voices
and lights and lives and music
and food and animals –
but I couldn't make myself heard
poor soul
couldn't make myself heard

Finally, my spirit exhausted,
I lay down on the air
and let myself lie loose
and nothing happened for quite a time
quite a long white time full of nothing until

I felt myself drifting down the street
and out of the town past the farthest houses
into a dimmish countryside
and swerving round the side of a bare hill
and into a deep forest

As I floated among the trees
I began to sing the song of a poor soul
and I could see that song fluttering in front of me
like a vermilion humming bird
and so I followed my songbird through the woods

I was surrounded by green
by a thousand shades of green
and gradually I found my song was joined
by other voices
so I smiled and looked up
and in the branches I saw perching
so many singing souls

And as I travelled from tree to tree
visiting the singing souls I found
that many of them were old friends of mine
and sometimes stayed holding each other's hands
to sing our hearts out for a time

And yet I always travelled on
and finally, in a grove of silver birches,
found my lost daughter
and my mother and my father

So here I perch
happily in the silver birches
singing with those I love our songs of love

Take your time, but when you're ready
come and join me in the silver birches.

Not Fleeing But Flying

I don't run away
But turn and stare
Into death's empty
Headlight glare

A take-off run
My wings unfold
Heartbeat wingbeat soaring
Up into the gold

Now if they ask you
Was I fleeing?
If they ask you
Was I crying?
If they ask you
Was I falling?
Tell em I was laughing
Tell em I was flying
Tell em I was sailing
Tell em I'm gone

In the Outlands

The Ballad of the Familiar Stranger

Well the sun was whiskey-yeller
And the tumbleweed was still
And the stubble sprouted blue upon his jaw
As the charismatic gringo
Fixed me with his eyes and said:
I ain't never going to Dogwood any more

I was ten days out of Pecos
When my Chevvy hit a bull
Bust a windscreen lost a hubcap bent a door
What a man receives a man retrieves
So I pushed it back to town
But I'm never going to Dogwood any more

Well she stood thar like a cactus
And I trembled like a clown
While a steel guitar played *Speed Me to the Shore*
When you've found a hat that fits you
Then you might as well go home
But I'm never going to Dogwood any more

Now when I smell buckwheat pancakes
Or I hear some fancy dude
Imitating Donald Duck my heart feels sore
For the something in between us
Was too big for both of them
And I'm never going to Dogwood any more.

So pass the Chivas Regal
And the Penthouse for July
If I slide right down this wall I'll find the floor
I got teardrops on my moustache
Armadillos in my jeans
And I'm never going to Dogwood any more

There's a kid in Sacramento
With a phone book on his head
There's a vulture with a big toe in its claw
There's a story-telling stranger
In the alcoholics ward
And he's never going to Dogwood
No he's never going to Dogwood
They won't let him into Dogwood any more

(This song should be punctuated by the whistle of a lonesome train in the distance.
Should an encore be called for, the audience deserve the following)

There's a Mayor in Zalamea
There's a Mill upon the Floss
There is punishment and crime and peace and war
Well they say that Michael Jackson
Is the Shadow Peter Pan
And I'm never going to Dogwood any more

Tables Tables Tables

M. Poussin found the card table covered with dead flies

as Alison entered the room,
eighty people in armour rose from
the long oak table and saluted her mischievously

put your head on my table

Matti asked to be buried with his favourite table

the chipped enamel of that kitchen table
forty-five summers ago
half-breaks my heart

the least popular table at the museum was Gerald's

on an orange tablecloth stained by many eggs
stood seventy jam jars full of mud from different rivers

on an egg tablecloth stained by many oranges
stood seventy mud jars full of pate from different livers

my heart is a table
and you done sawed off three of its legs

Bobby Kay was the only American in my mother's nursery school
so we hit him over the head with a table

the beauty of a billiards table
which has nothing to say but: Play

you will all stay here in the Hall until the boy owns up
who was responsible for losing the eighty-seven times table

Transmogrification

We went to the Gasleak Party
We queued for a smell of the Wall
We each took a sniff and turned yellowy–green
And woke up six inches tall

Gerald Stimpson's Safety First Songbook

Pullover Perils

When your auntie knits you a pullover
And you pull it over
DO stick your head through the hole
Provided for your head!
Should you force your head
Down one of the armholes
You may stretch the knitting
And squash your nose
And, in the pullover darkness, blind as an onion,
Bump into a bus
Or fall down a canyon!

Television Hazards

It's fun fun fun
Life with a television set!
You see such wonderful things!
And you ain't seen nothing yet!
But remember what Mr Safety First says:
Don't get your TV wet!

Don't pour pints of bitter on your telly!
Don't empty jugs of water on it!
Don't throw bottles of milk at your telly!
And please don't piddle upon it!

Old Mother Chaos
(Mother of the First Man)

Old Mother Chaos –
Spectacular woman –
Bit like a compost heap
Of ostrich feathers.
Lost civilisations dangling
From the tendrils of her armpits,
Lips crawling with crocodiles
And a hundred bosoms swinging
Like the Count Basie Band
Serving hot milk, cold milk, chocolate milk,
Banana milk shakes and vodka martinis
As her feet blap-slapped out a bluesy beat
Across the celestial linoleum.

Old Mother Chaos –
Marvellous woman –
Got a bit famous
When she laid that Cosmic Egg
Which bust in half
To form the Earth and Sky
And – slap-bang in the middle of the two halves –
    P'AN KU
The First Man
Lolling on a new–laid carpet of moss
Looking astounded at everybloodything,
Especially himself.

Old Mother Chaos
Hellpat of a woman –
Bumped into her once
Schlepping round the Silky Way.
About P'An Ku, I said to her – Who?
You mean that funny TV penguin? she asked
No, I said, not Pingu, P'an Ku! Your son?
The First Man in Creation?
Oh him! How did he turn out? she asked.

I told her straight:
After he cracked out of that egg of yours
He started growing –
Every day he was ten feet taller.
Soon he would have hit the sky,

But every day the sky was ten feet taller,
Every day the earth was ten feet thicker,

Old Mother Chaos –
Wonder of a woman –
Asked: What's my boy up to now?
Sorry, I said, but when P'An Ku
Was 18,000 years old and – let me see –
65 million 700 thousand feet tall –
He tripped over his pet tortoise,
Toppled and bust his brainbox
On the mantelpiece of the Himalayas.

He never! He did.
His head split in two bits
And they became the sun and moon.
Blood flowing everywhere,
Filling up the riverbeds and oceanbeds.
His hair turned into
The trees of the forest and the meadow grass.
His sweat became the rain,
His breath the wind,
His voice the thunder
And his fleas –
The ancestors of the human race.

Old Mother Chaos –
Wicked old woman –
Said: He turned out like his father, then.
Who was that?, I asked.
Bloke I met in a pub –
Sort of half catfish,
Half dragon,
Half pyramid,
Half millipede –
All shook up in a bin-bag,
You know the sort.

This dude spouted the usual routine –
How his brain's been wonky
Ever since the war between
The Geometrical Twins
And the Gaslight Cherrybangs.
Mainly I felt sorry for him,
Well, you know me – archetypal old softy.

Yeah – it was in The Flighty Mucklebeast –
An inter-Galactic Scottish theme pub
On the 723rd moon of Saturn.

Old Mother Chaos –
Whirlwind of a woman –
Kept on spinning her yarn to me,
All the time tickling my arrangements
With her multiplex fingerprints
And elastaploid nippletips
Till I was rolling round the womb of the void –
But the rest of this story is unrepeatable –
At least in human company

Every Day Is Mothering Sunday to Me

The sea is mother to the shore
The scalp is mother to the hair
The bread is mother to the butter
The table is mother to the chair
The town is mother to the country
The zoo is mother to the bear

    Come down to the Mother Market
    Millions of Mothers are on view
    Their smiles shine down the mile-long aisles
And there on a shelf is the perfect Mother for you

Oh seek her and take her by her motherly hand
She steps into your silvery shopping cart
Pay at the till the amount on her label
And wheel her out of the Mother Mart

But should you be still dissatisfied
Fill in our Mother–Cover–Guarantee
And you'll be shipped another Mother
From the Mother Factory.

Adult Fairy-tale

This is the story of little red riding hump she got a little red when
she was riding but boy could she hump

Another Invitation to Another Committee

The Access Committee for Security
Is holding a meeting tonight
We're meeting at my place because of the Fog
So I'm hoping that the Agamatic lights

Mr Griddlestone is bringing his favourite ashtray
Mrs Benefit will be radiant in aubergine
The Lograboff Twins are turning up late
They're finishing a marble ladder for the Queen

And the Chair of the Committee asked me to say
That we'll all be expecting you
The Agenda may look quite horrific
But Any Other Business may bring
A pleasant surprise or two

Well meetings drag on as meetings will
Just listen to the Colonel's moustache
The portraits on the walls begin to melt into yawns
And your thoughts are gradually turning to ash

But it's fearfully urgent all the same
Despite those moments of rage or shame
And I'm sure that you're going to be glad you came
And one thing I promise you

One thing I promise you
When you leave the meeting of the Access Committee
Things won't be the same
You won't be the same
You won't ever be the same again

Jungle Businessman Snapshot

Across those treacherous liana bridges,
To work he plods, at seven on the dot.
Bitten by conscience and by midges,
Watched by a flatulent ocelot.

Rosaura's Song

Dreamed I was the lover
Of a beautiful thief
But when I woke up
I was a shipwreck on a reef.
Dreamed that I was happy
Or so it seemed to seem.
My lover smiled
Like a clown in a dream.

A clown in a dream
A clown in a dream
I had a dream
We were clowns in a dream.

Dreamed I was a husband
Dreamed I was a wife
But when I woke up
I wanted vengeance with a knife.
Dreamed I was the knife
And blood began to stream
But when I woke up
I was a clown in a dream.

A clown in a dream
Failing upside down
And when I woke up
I was a dream in a clown.

(from Calderon's *Life's a Dream*)

The Phunny Phallus Phellow

One
was such fun
that I grew
Two

Philosophical Agriculture

The Cow of Friedrich Nietzsche
was a recalcitrant creature
who kicked Rainer Maria Rilke
whenever he tried to milk her

Time to Vertigo

When I meditate on the Zillennium
Or mull over a micro-minute
My stomach feels like an enormous fridge
With nothing in it.

Flouncing Out

Me and my Gnome
Are going home to Rome
And we'll never come back to your Aerodrome

The Knife–thrower's Slender Daughter

The Knife-thrower's slender daughter
Sent me a letter one day
Meet me just above the forest
Daddy's going to be away
All day
Daddy's going to be away

I climbed up the path to the forest
And – sitting astride a log –
I saw the Knife–thrower feeding
Egg and bacon to his one–eyed dog
I did
Egg and bacon to his one–eyed dog

The first three knives he threw at me
I dodged his every shot
Then his one-eyed dog ran past me
And retrieved the bloody lot
He did
Retrieved the bloody lot

Well I started throwing bits of brick and stone
Cos the blades fell around me like rain
But they bounced off the Knife-thrower's helmet
And he started in to throw again
Damn him
And the dog retrieved the knives again

I seemed to see him in close-up
Intense and stony-eyed
And the rocks I chucked didn't reach him
He was further up the mountainside
With the dog
Further up the mountain side

Well the Knife-thrower's slender daughter
Looked down to the valley road
And she saw a blue and white cop car
Sitting there like a toad
So she took a little hatchet from her hip
She gave it a swing
And she gave it a flip
And the hatchet flew like a meteorite
And smashed into the cop car's revolving light

The cops switched on their siren
And I heard their engine roar
And zooming up from the valley
Came the forces of the Law
With pistols
Came the forces of the Law

They locked up the Knife-thrower
For six months and a day
With his daughter and his one-eyed dog
I made my getaway
You know
And here's all I want to say

Now I don't blame the Knife-thrower or his dog
For protecting his daughter from me
And if you saw Knife-thrower's slender daughter
You sureashell wouldn't blame me
Oh no
You sureashell wouldn't blame me.

On board the FRIENDSHIP

For Dick and Dixie Peaslee

my friends and I
are trees in a wood
we glory in autumn's
goldenhood

on our branches sing
the owl and the lark
and the small deer trot
through the mist for our bark

and the river below
runs silvery-grey
with barges to carry
the timber away

and that voyage to the ocean
seems happy and good
to me and my friends
as we dance in our wood

How William Blake Dies a Good Death

(for John McGrath)

It was a summer evening.
The window was wide open.
I was sixty-nine
And I'd been ill for months.
I was sitting propped up in our bed and drawing.

I said: Stay Kate, keep just as you are,
I will draw you
For you have ever been an angel to me.
I drew her lovely face.

Then I put down my pencil and said:
Kate, I am a changing man.
At night I often rose and wrote down my thoughts,
Whether it rained or snowed or shone,
And you arose and sat beside me
And held my left hand as I wrote my poems.
This can be no longer.

And then I made up a song
And sang it, quietly, into Kate's ear.
And then another song
And then another.

And Kate said: I like your songs.
So I said: They are not mine,
My beloved, they are not mine.

I took one last breath of the summer air
And let it go
And my life flew out of the window
And upwards, singing joyfully.

Two Daffodils for Adrian Henri

Just a Gift

Wanted to bring a present to your funeral.
All I could find was this.
Look Adrian –
A mugful of snow.

Tastes good.

Just a Closer Walk with Adrian

Adrian out for a country walk
Through Liverpool and Paris.
Bursting eclairs and cream slices
Shining in the hedgerows.

Adrian followed his luminous dong
Into the municipal park called Eden.
Under the monkey-puzzle tree
Stood Catherine Marcangeli.

Her name was a poem,
Her eyes were poems
And her voice was a river of poetry
As she sang,
With a perfect Franco-Italian accent
That most beautiful of recitations:

There's a famous seaside place called Blackpool
That's noted for fresh air and fun,
And Mr and Mrs Ramsbottom
Went there with young Albert, their son...

Yes, Shakespeare's Albert and the Lion!
This lowly bit of holy writ
With its rolly-poly wit
Reduced the Bard of Birkenhead to the state
Of a chest-tickled moggie
Or a gurgling Ubu
With a deep magical delight
Which lasted fifteen years,
Which lasts forever.

For Miranda and Tom

(two babies who did not live long)

a handful of days
a handful of daisies
floating down a piano-playing river

o life is so little
far too little
but love flies on for ever

David in the Waterpark

where the sun watches its double image on the screen of the reservoir

where the pink grandchild with a woolly top totters like a newborn foal

where ferns curl up and out of the dark undergrowth
   holding up their round hands to catch the light

where free water presses kisses on the edge of the breathing ice

where the tractor-ploughman whistles his spiralling rhapsody

where the frost white feather is united with the feather white frost

   he lay on his back on the hard green bank

      singing like a wild red sweater

Roses in the Summertime Rain

A Wedding Poem for Heather and Paul

Now the Mersey river has a Mississippi beat
keeps his eyes on Ireland as he surges so strong.
River Tyne shakes her bridges like bracelets:
And I heard them singing this wedding song –

People you love, they're the real things,
only thing that's left when everything goes wrong.
People you love, they're the real things,
only thing left when the world goes wrong.
      When one good person
    finds another good person –
that's a blackbird song, a magical song,
and all your friends here and gone
    want to sing along.

     all we need is
   all kinds of love
     deep love
  comforting love
    wild love
  and wise love

 So if you find a lover
who's a good warm woman like Heather –
    If you find a lover
who's a good warm man like Paul.
    If you find a lover
with the honest to goodness
    of a real good dog –
       that's good
         so good
well we knew that you would!

     all we need is
   all kinds of love
   love of friends
   love of family
   love of animals
   love of a lover
   love of our world
   love of peace

            Paul gave us songs
made us feel we were building
Blake's New Jerusalem here and now –
      that's a generous kind of love
      Heather took her suffering
Then shook off that suffering
to help the wretched of the earth –
      that's a brave kind of love

            He has walked across
                  frozen lands of loss
      She has staggered through
                  deserts of pain
      They could have stayed alone
They could have turned to stone
      but they turned to each other
            and they grew together
      May their happiness shine
like roses in the summertime rain

Because people you love they're the real things
only thing left when everything goes wrong
People you love they're the real things
only thing left when everything goes wrong
            when one good person
      finds another good person –
that's a blackbird song, a magical song,
and all your loves here and gone
            let them sing along
and may your Newcastle Liverpool love keep singing
            man and wife all your golden life
      and may that life be lovely

            as a golden retriever
in the wildwoods of autumn

            as bright woollen children
      riding scarlet toboggans

            as unicorns dancing
      down the meadows of April

as roses in the summertime rain.

(June 11th 2002)

The Granite Gift

(for Ivor Cutler on his 80th birthday)

because your music
squeezes from the harmless harmonium
like orange from a juice

because your eyebrows
stand sentry duty over your eyes
like two families of alert meerkats
supervising a couple of lochs

because your words
have the daft wisdom
of Edward Satie and Erik Lear
and the delicious grace
of a Japanese water deer

because your smile
delights my heart

I have started to make a present
for your Eighty Bird Day

it will be a bicycle
carved from the living granite

each wheel shall be fitted
with eighty spokes
fashioned from stalactites
and stalagmites
and stalagoofs

the handlebars of your granite bicycle
shall be very nice
what with diamonds and emeralds
and wine-gums embedded
in the antlers of an obliging moose

what about the saddle?
I hear you ask –
it shall be of firm and sensuous
sumptuous silk –
astride that saddle shall be seated
a spiced and sultry sweetmeat

of an Indian dancing girl
especially enamoured of thee
with dark and googly eyes she shall entice thee
saying: Ivor come mount your bicycle
for I am thy saddle

and as you ride that granite bike
across the cloudways of Old Europe
all creatures great and small shall sing:
Hey, look at that sparkling Scottish Bard
on his sparkling granite bike!

PS but I have to confess
I have not made much progress up to now
in the creation of your granite bike
your beautiful bike your spiritual bike
your bike of wonder your birthday bike,
I have done some you know preliminary thinking

and I did find a piece of granite
in a heap of Camden gravel

but it fell out through a hole
in my trousers pocket

maybe next year

A Song for Maeve

I love to watch rivers
and the way they go
young rivers tumble
old rivers flow

I love to watch friends
when they're letting go –
the tumbling laughter
and the story flow

and the words sweet Maeve uses
with such gaiety
go tumbling and flowing
to join the great sea

Seventy More Years
(for Gordon Snell on his birthday)

I was fifteen, and shaking.
I'd been asked to write the House Play
And I'd said yes and now I was terrified.
I couldn't do it alone, so I sought you out
Because I'd heard you'd written a dozen plays
For your own puppet theatre.

You were fifteen too.
As I spoke to you for the first time
You looked at me as if I were
An intriguing painting, by Breughel maybe,
Listened to my invitation
And smiled Yes.
What had I taken on?
In the gym and at rugby you were agile as an ape,
But I could tolerate some sportiness.
The prefects had you down as Trouble,
With a deadly line in Dumb Insolence
And a reputation as the eloquent School Atheist.
Well, that was fine with me,
Speaking as a close friend of the School Communist
And a loose troupe of jazz fanatics.

We walked and talked and sat down and laughed
As we plotted our blockbuster for the Drama Competition.
Half an hour long said the rules, and we knew that
To impress our toffee-tough audience of teenage boys
The play better have a lot about Death.

And so we wrote *A Friend of Ours* –
In which Death himself, an old man in a wheelchair
Wearing Matron's black and scarlet cloak,
Invites a job-lot of odd guests to his country house.
A Sailor, a Scientist, a Poet (me) and –
You as Miss Marguerite Hyde – described as a Traveller.
Death accuses Miss Hyde of nameless crimes
And she replies with this interior monologue:
'I've met the danger of death before,
But it's always been a danger I could fight –
In the East one can fight the terrors of the jungle but this…
I never reckoned with having to fight Death 'in person'.

To think that old man has the power to end anyone's life,
Anyone's at all – to end mine.
To think HE is Death – It almost seems absurd –
But it's not funny.
How can I fight Death?...

Did we win the play competitions
By ten lengths and a carrot!
We always won.
You and I took turns to win the Poetry Competition
And the best parts in the School Shakespeare production.
When I played justice Shallow, you were Doll Tearsheet.
When you played a dazzling Hamlet,
I was your grumpy Uncle Claudius.

Only once failure seemed to loom. Instead of a tragedy
We entered a farce for the Play Competition –
The Third Ham – a parody of the Harry Lime movie
With my Trevor Howard, your Orson Welles.
But the censorship committee banned our entry
For blasphemy and obscenity.
We glared at them and exited,
Sat down and wrote another tragedy – *Dead End*.

Its first stage direction reads:
'David Hayes is seated, alone and rather dishevelled.'
(No wonder, he has been shot at by the police
And is dying of his wounds in a warehouse).
His opening blank verse monologue was spoken by me,
But written, I would claim, mainly by Gordon.

'Cobwebs cast stealthy shadows in the soft dust
The weary bales loom dark against the warehouse wall
The black rain caresses the blank indifferent bricks...
I cannot see the steps that led to this dead end
I do not understand.
Bewildered, bewildered, there are mists about my eyes,
And I am dying without knowing the reason.
This bullet in my stomach is my life's result,
The culmination of the sequence of my acts,
A sequence I must try to follow...
How did it all begin?...
How did it all begin?...'

Did we win the Competition?
Does the Pope shit in the woods?

Pausing only to re–cycle *The Third Ham*
As a cowboy epic called *Cow–Cow Bogey*
In which we played the Front and Back halves
Of the mooing, Charleston–dancing heroine,
We founded the Symbolic Society
Which improvised weird and subversive plays
On the verandah of the cricket pavilion
To an audience of moonlit grass.

And together we sat in the great secret attic
Up above the Farmer Hall,
Discussing Love and War and Thurber and Duke Ellington
Seated in enormous wooden Shakespeare thrones
Puffing at our Park Drives
And laughing ourselves into a kind of
Heaven of understanding.

Together we cycled across Wiltshire
To a weekend school on the poetry of John Donne
Whom we'd never heard of
Then J.B. Leishmann burst into the lecture room
With a bicycle and Mickey Mouse hair
And began to read aloud to us
But after two lines threw down the book
And carried on by heart:

'Go and catch a falling star,
Get with child a mandrake root,
Tell me where all past years are
Or who cleft the devil's foot.

Teach me to hear mermaids singing,
Or to keep off envy's stinging,
And find
What wind
Serves to advance an honest mind.'

And we glanced at each other,
Realising that Donne was of our gang,
And, cycling back to school,
Chanted the words of Donne,
Laughing with love
For his daft and dangerous language.

Called up to do National Stupidity in the RAF
We squarebashed side by side
Trying to keep each other sane
In that insane little world of blanco, bootpolish
And being broke and bullied –
Always you were my ideal friend.

When you were promoted to be an Acting Corporal –
It seemed, at first, a betrayal –
Had Snell joined the Establishment?
But no, within weeks you had been shorn of your chevrons,
Demoted back to my humble level
For bureaucratic sabotage.

On leave, tramping over Lakeland
We rewrote its literary history
In a musical movie called *The Road to Keswick*
Starring Bing Crosby as Wordsworth,
Bob Hope as Coleridge,
Dorothy Lamour as Dorothy Wordsworth
And Louis Armstrong as the Leech Gatherer
And endless fantasy melodramas
Most of them building to a Rabelaisian climax
Involving all the Windsor–Mountbattens.

You went to Balliol, I went to Christ Church.
At Oxford, our adventure playground.
Every night we were walking on the rooftops
Or using your room as a basketball court
For a balloon version of the game
Played with a beer in one hand.
We acted, we wrote poems and stories,
We founded the Universal Monster Club
Which turned up at movies like
The Creature from the Black Lagoon
To cheer the monster and hiss the awful actors…
We have heard the chimes at midnight, Master Gordon…
But you actually worked and won a good degree
And landed up in the BBC
And there were Bush House sessions
And Twite and Dromgoole
And Moira and Annie
And Bruce and O'Toole
And high above the streets of Earls Court
The laughter circus of your flat in Hogarth Road.

We found ourselves the only inhabitants
Of a caravan site on the Gower Peninsula
In the depths of a Bible-black winter
Trying to write a sitcom about
A troupe of nutty actors in a theatre on a pier
But continually breaking away from work
For trips to the cliffside pub
Or our own madly competitive
Two–man Olympic Games
With events like Sand Dune Jumping Downwards,
Tossing the Boulder and
The Walking Backwards Into the Sea Race.
After each event we stood on the caravan steps,
The loser on the lower step,
For the presentation of gold and silver medals
Fashioned from Barley Wine bottle top wrappers,
To sing the winner's National Anthem…

And it was all very wild and wonderful
But there was something the matter with the weather
Something the matter with the light –
The work was fine
And the fun and the friendship were fine
But love arrived and threw her arms around you sometimes,
Stayed awhile,
Then, painfully, left.

That's not enough love for a man
When the greatest among his many talents
Is a huge gift for loving others.
Love is tough stuff, and it was tough of love to be so mean
To the most generous man in the world.

But the world turned
And the weather changed to summertime
And the monochrome streets
Were suddenly bright
With all the colours sunshine paints on London,
With all the music sunshine plays on Dublin.
And you sailed away, for a year and a day,
In a beautiful pea–green sieve
And magic-carpeted round the globe –
What a runcible way to live!
And you sat in a tree–top side by side
By the light of the Chablis sun,
Writing green and blossoming poems
And stories for everyone.

131

Maeve and Gordon,
Gordon and Maeve,
Two names which sit together
Like two loving cats in an armchair.
Beauty meeting beauty,
It was so clear, so happy,
So unconditionally
For ever.

Maeve and Gordon
Gordon and Maeve,
Your deep joy shines
All around you
Warming the hearts
Of your numberless friends,
Warming us all
With your deep joy.

For ever
For ever
Flowing like a river –
Your love and your deep joy.

SEVENTY MORE YEARS!

to all our friends

August
blue seas for ever
a spicy breeze
bears us towards an ancient island

the harbour opens its arms to us
in an embrace
of boats with clinking masts
brown children leaping over ropes
donkeys fishermen dogs
women with baby bundles
shadow cats
and the sun
shining down upon a maze
of whitewashed alleys
leading up towards
bright domes and shining towers
and beyond all these
the dark hills of enchantment

we have come home
to the island which we've been creating
for so many years
with our buckets and spades

and here we all stand
with salt spray in our eyes
makers of dreamcakes and mudpies

Books available by Adrian Mitchell

POETRY

Love Songs of World War Three (Allison & Busby/W.H. Allen, 1989)
Greatest Hits: His 40 Golden Greats (Bloodaxe Books, 1991)
Blue Coffee: Poems 1985-1996 (Bloodaxe Books, 1996)
Heart on the Left: Poems 1953-1984 (Bloodaxe Books, 1997)
All Shook Up: Poems 1997-2000 (Bloodaxe Books, 2000)
The Shadow Knows: Poems 2000-2004 (Bloodaxe Books, 2004)

PLAYS

The Pied Piper (Oberon Books)
Gogol: The Government Inspector (Methuen)
Calderón: The Mayor of Zalamea & two other plays (Absolute Classics)
Lope de Vega: Fuente Ovejuna and Lost in a Mirror (Absolute Classics)
Tyger Two, Man Friday, Satie Day/Night and *In the Unlikely Event
    of an Emergency* (Oberon Books)
The Siege (Oberon Books)
The Snow Queen (Oberon Books)
The Mammoth Sails Tonight! (Oberon Books)
The Lion, the Witch and the Wardrobe (Oberon Books)
The Mammoth Sails Tonight (Oberon Books)
Alice in Wonderland and Through the Looking Glass (Oberon Books)
Peter Rabbit and His Friends (Oberon Books)

POETRY FOR CHILDREN

The Orchard Book of Poems (Orchard, 1993)
The Thirteen Secrets of Poetry (Macdonald, 1993)
Balloon Lagoon (Orchard, 1997)
Dancing in the Street (Orchard, 1999)
Daft as a Doughnut (Orchard, 2004)

CHILDREN'S STORIES

The Ugly Duckling (Dorling Kindersley)
The Steadfast Tin Soldier (Dorling Kindersley)
Maudie and the Green Children (Tradewind)
Nobody Rides the Unicorn (Transworld)
My Cat Mrs Christmas (Orion)
The Adventures of Robin Hood and Marian (Bloomsbury)
Twice My Size (Orchard Books)

RECORDINGS

The Dogfather (57 Productions – double CD)

For more information, check out www.adrianmitchell.co.uk